Discover the "Secret Formula" that the Most
Successful Local Businesses Use
to Fuel Growth and Outperform the Competition

Cracking The Code Of
Local Business Growth

Welcome

What I'm about to show you can ignite growth at your business well beyond the levels you've likely achieved in the past.

How do I know this is true?

Because 95 percent of the clients I have worked with over the years are missing AT LEAST two out of the four critical, proven marketing systems that are necessary to achieve maximum business growth.

And the clients who are leveraging all four? They're growing. *Fast.*

So unless your situation is completely out of the ordinary (which is possible but unlikely), ***there is a really big opportunity to accelerate the growth of your business***.

And the acceleration I'm talking about isn't a short-lived "sugar-rush" kind of growth. It's the sustainable and responsible kind—the kind that complements your ethical standards and supports your long-term vision for your business.

Skeptical?

I understand. But as you continue reading, you'll discover that the systems I'm talking about aren't gimmicky, revolutionary or impossible to implement. They don't require you to turn your business model upside down or become something you're not.

In fact, *these four elements are the foundational building blocks that every successful business must optimize in order to achieve the growth they're looking fo*r. But again, my experience tells me that most businesses are not taking complete (or efficient) advantage of each of the four pieces.

About The Author

Olivier Glaudy is the Chief Marketing Officer at Roar Marketing Consultants a digital marketing agency based in Houston, Tx that helps local businesses and professionals with their online marketing and presence, online reputation marketing, Google Adwords management and social media marketing.

Olivier is an expert in marketing, and specifically local marketing. He leverages technology to achieve maximum results, so that his clients can focus on what they do best:

Sell their products and services.

Olivier Glaudy has been cited in major national news channels websites such as Fox,CBS,NBC, ABC, etc…

You can enjoy his marketing tips and insights by following him on Twitter & Periscope @olivierglaudy or by connecting with him on Linkedin.

Table Of Content

Chp 1: The 3 Dramatic Changes in the Marketplace In the Last 10 Years

The competitive landscape for local businesses has changed drastically. Especially over the last 10 years, we've seen dramatic changes in the way that we do business due to software, the Internet and technology, and it will continue to change at an unprecedented pace.

The landscape has changed and so has the means your customers find and shop for products or your services. The continued development and distribution of technology has radically changed the way consumers are buying—how they hear about products and services; how they research them; and how they make a final purchase decision.

Regrettably, I found that businesses in general and 95% of small businesses in particular, across almost any vertical industry, have been slow to adapt to these changes, and consequently are losing at least two out of the four marketing systems we're going to cover in this book that are crucial to attain maximum growth.

We are going to cover what those major changes are and we're going to talk about the important systems you should make certain that you have in place to capitalize on these changes. So, what are the three large drivers of change that I mentioned?

Well, they are--

1 Search
2 Social
3 Mobile

I'm confident these are all terms that you're familiar with; however, you might not be just acquainted with how these matters are impacting your business, your consumers' want to do business with you and the conclusions you have to make at your business to make sure that you are capitalizing on these changes.

1.Search

Search engines did not even exist 15 years ago, now they are only a part of the manner every single day that we run. It's simpler more than ever to find advice about products, services, businesses, individuals, places or whatever it is the fact that you're seeking. Search engines now are reachable from multiple devices. Search can be accessed by us from our smartphones and, obviously, from iPads our computers or tablet computers now when we're walking or driving. So, information actually has become amazingly accessible as well as the search engines have become the predominant way that people now find advice about those company and products.

It is no longer the yellow pages it's search engines. In fact, 92% of consumers have more confidence in the info located than they do in anything from other source or a sales clerk. In other words is not only are we finding our information online, but we really trust it more than the information we get directly from companies and that makes sense. When information is coming from a company directly we feel like they are selling us or advertising to us, so we have more religion in the information than we do from advice directly from businesses that we find with search engines.

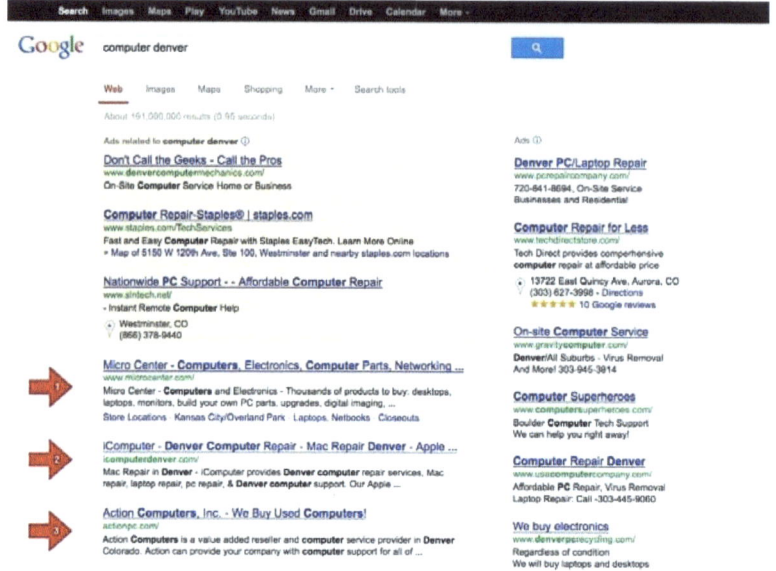

*According to Google, 97 percent of consumers search for **local** businesses online. The top 10 organic (non-paid) search results get 95 percent of the clicks.*

First, a look at the numbers. According to recent poll data from the Pew Internet and American Life Project, 92 percent of adult Internet users in the U.S. use a search engine (e.g. Google, Bing) to find information online—with the majority of this group performing keyword searches on a regular basis.

When you look at educated and affluent individuals, search engine use climbs to as high as 98 percent.

These statistics simply underline what you and I already know: **Search is King**.

Everyone who has access to the Internet uses a search engine to find relevant and useful information, and according to Google's own data, 97 percent of consumers search for **local** businesses online.

Got visibility?

The upshot of these facts is clear: If you want visibility for your business, you need visibility in the search engines, particularly Google.

Search isn't just king—it's a kingmaker too. High visibility in Google can mean more website traffic, more customers and referrals, more sales activity, and more profit for your business.

And for those business owners in hyper-competitive markets, search-engine visibility can be the difference between being an unknown also-ran and being the Top Dog.

The good, the bad and the ugly: there for all to see

But visibility is a double-edged sword. Customer reviews of your business are visible too.

What if some of these reviews are negative?

What if they're *scathing*?

Well, the bad news is they can haunt your business for years and have a crushing impact on your bottom line.

On the flip side, good reviews can fuel positive word of mouth and generate referral traffic like you've never seen!

Ranking matters

Here's what we know about how people use search engines: after entering a keyword into Google and being presented with pages and pages of blue text links, consumers generally don't dive very deeply into the results (95.91 percent of all clicks occur on page one).

And of page one results, people tend to focus on the top three. According to an Optify study, the top three positions for any given term account for nearly 60 percent (58.5) of the traffic. The top result alone commands an average click-through rate (CTR) of 36.4 percent.

So it's not enough to be "on Google." If you want to take advantage of the popularity of search, your website needs to be listed at the top of the page and above the "scroll line" for the search terms relevant to your business.

2. Social

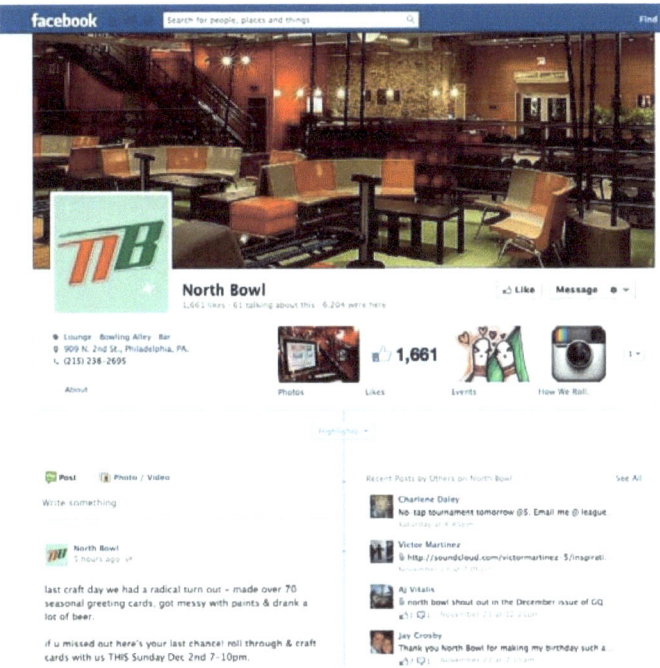

Small businesses have (finally) embraced social media. According to HubSpot, 90 percent of small businesses are on Facebook, and 66 percent of them are spending more time on social media than they did a year ago.

The social web has truly been a game changer. Now, social is the second important factor and if search engines have grown rapidly, nicely then social media websites are just absolutely on fire. It's amazing the increase in societal. The social web has truly been a game changer.

Linking and sharing with others, sharing our views with others, has never been so easy and those opinions are highly observable. People spend a great deal of time in the search engines each day, with them is very, quite visible, so what's being shared and now part of people's everyday lives.

 The important thing you must know about this is the fact that it's easier than ever for individuals to create and share information about how they feel about your company, products and services.

You are not mainly creating the content about your business that is out there on the Web . It's the consumers which are the publishers of that advice and that is a major, major impact on how we do business.

Just think: Facebook grew from a curiosity in a Harvard dormitory to a global force with over 1,000,000,000 users … in less than a decade.

Facebook seems like old news now—a presence in our lives that we take for granted—but it's worth remembering how recently this shift has taken place.

Actually, take a look at this statistic. Seventy percent of consumers consult with ratings or reviews on-line before purchasing. That comes from a file called Zero Moment of Truth that was released by Google in 2011. So, societal is having a huge effect on how people make buying choices.

70% of consumers consult reviews or ratings *BEFORE* **purchasing.**

Google Zero Moment of Truth 2011

Not just for kids

A common misunderstanding that small businesses have is that Facebook and other networks are just for kids, and thus their target market isn't represented demographically on the site.

But the stats tell another story—the opposite story, in fact.

In the U.S., almost two-thirds of all Facebook users are over the age of 35. Recent Pew research reveals that **two-thirds** of U.S. adults use social networking sites like Facebook and Twitter.

High engagement

People aren't just ON social networks. They're GLUED to them.

The average U.S. Facebook user spends a whopping **7 hours and 46 minutes on the site each month**.

That's a full 15.5 minutes the average American spends on Facebook every single day!

The upshot of all of these numbers is pretty straightforward, but I'll spell it out just in case:

Your customers are on Facebook.

They spend a LOT of time there. They're sharing, tweeting, liking, pinning, friending, starring, following, fanning, posting, hash tagging, uploading, retweeting … you name it.

So if you want to reach them, capture their attention and make a pitch for your services before your competitors do … you've got to at least meet them halfway.

Sharing experiences … and frustrations

People are taking to the web to share their experiences with brands, and what they're sharing with their friends and family members isn't always flattering …

According to a study from the [Society for Communications Research](), 59 percent of U.S. consumers are using social media to **vent** about customer care frustrations. This isn't just happening on Facebook, but on sites like Angie's List, Yelp, Google+ Local and others. According to research from Deloitte & Touche, **7 in 10** who read reviews **share** them with friends, family and colleagues, amplifying the impact of these comments even further.

Study: 59 percent of U.S. consumers use social media to vent about customer care frustrations.

More and more businesses are beginning to realize that, while they can't control what people say online, they can (and should) monitor and contribute to the conversation in an effort to influence the overall tenor.

They're realizing that having a **proactive online presence** that's focused on **adding value to the customer experience** is the surest way to grow and preserve their brand reputation—and protect themselves from the stray musings of a few unhappy souls.

Keeping pace with buyer expectations

Another big reason to get involved in social media is that you have to do it to **stay relevant**.

Your buyers expect it, and if you fall short of their expectations, they'll be more likely to spend their money with the guy down the street.

Even way back in 2008, a Cone Business study on social media found that **93 percent of customers expected companies to have a presence on social channels**, and **85 percent expected companies to interact with them on those social channels**.

That figure has only grown as the social media era has matured.

You can either join the conversation or let your competitors do all the talking.

It's up to you!

3. Mobile ("The really, really big one")

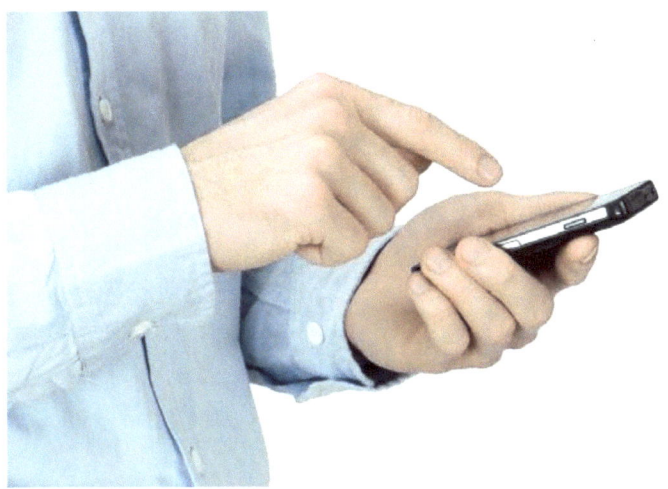

According to research from Mobile Marketer, 70 percent of all mobile searches result in action within one hour!

The 3rd major variable is cellular and this may be the largest game changer of all. Well, it was one thing when we had access to all of this amazing info on our computers, but the truth is that a lot of folks aren't sitting at their computers twenty-four hours a day.

They are up and about, traveling around town, going to meetings or whatever it's they are doing, shopping. Now most people have accessibility to any or all of this info in the palm of their hands wherever they are at and they're using it.

Mobile search gives that immediate gratification people are searching for, so if you are not present on mobile and in case you do not understand how people's buying behavior is changing, your opponents will eat your lunch.

Actually, have a look at the statistics. One in seven searches are now mobile. You add all of this up and it's simpler than ever for consumer to quickly study and compare various services and products.

Mobile searches have QUADRUPLED in the last year according to Google.**1 in 7** searches are now mobile.

This is a screen shot from a site called Trip Advisor that I am sure many of you've been to. I know for me, personally, when we travel and intend a vacation Trip Advisor is the place I spend a lot of time doing my research and it really, really has an impact on the conclusions I make about the places that I want to stay. So, Trip Advisor and some sites that were similar has radically impacted the hospitality industry, but it's not just the hospitality industry it is all industries.

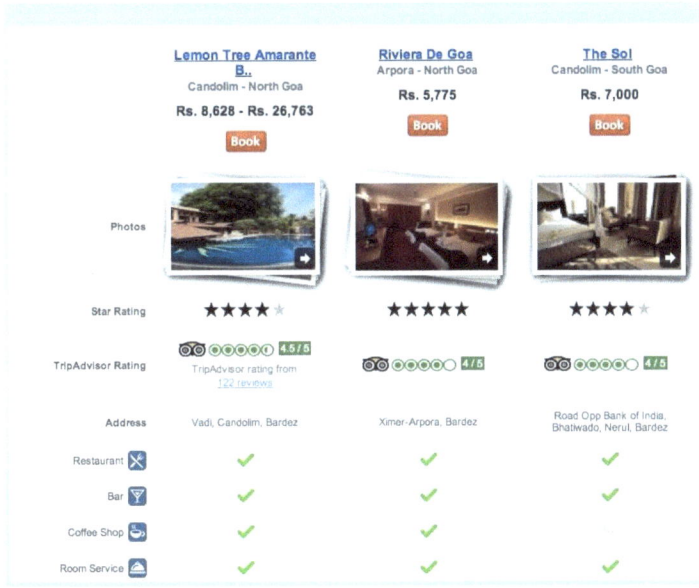

	Lemon Tree Amarante B..	Riviera De Goa	The Sol
	Candolim - North Goa	Arpora - North Goa	Candolim - South Goa
	Rs. 8,628 - Rs. 26,763	Rs. 5,775	Rs. 7,000
	Book	Book	Book
Photos			
Star Rating	★★★★☆	★★★★★	★★★★☆
TripAdvisor Rating	⊙⊙ ⊙⊙⊙⊙⊙ 4.5/5 TripAdvisor rating from 122 reviews	⊙⊙ ⊙⊙⊙⊙○ 4/5	⊙⊙ ⊙⊙⊙⊙○ 4/5
Address	Vadi, Candolim, Bardez	Ximer-Arpora, Bardez	Road Opp Bank of India, Bhatwado, Nerul, Bardez
Restaurant	✔	✔	✔
Bar	✔	✔	✔
Coffee Shop	✔	✔	
Room Service	✔	✔	✔

Look around you: You'll see a steady stream of consumers surfing the web on smartphones, iPads, Nooks, and Kindles.

And this is a trend that's hardly slowing.

It's almost impossible to overestimate the impact of the mobile computing revolution.

In fact, the proliferation of cellphones, smartphones, e-readers and tablet PCs might be one of the most **underestimated** and **under-hyped** shifts in business today.

Today, 87 percent of Americans have mobile phones. It's their No. 1 most-used technology device, with 73 percent saying so versus only 58 percent saying it's their desktop PC.

In their recent Mobile Internet Report, Morgan Stanley projects that mobile browsing will outpace desktop-based access within 3–5 years.

When you pause to consider what these newfangled devices are capable of, and how quickly they emerged from high-priced novelties to ever-present, "can't live without them"[1] gadgets ... it's pretty unbelievable.

Marc Andreessen, co-creator of Netscape, the first widely used web browser, adds some helpful perspective: "We have never lived in a time with the opportunity to put a computer in the pocket of 5 billion people. Practically everyone is going to have a general purpose computer in their pocket, it's so easy to underestimate that, that has got to be **the really, really big one**."

A recent article in the Economist adds this:

> "*The potential of the smartphone age is deceptive. We look around and see more people talking on phones in more places and playing Draw Something when they're bored.*

---

[1] To illustrate this point, consider this statistic from Unisys: It takes 26 hours for the average person to report a lost wallet. It takes only 68 minutes for them to report a lost phone.

This is just the beginning. In time, business models, infrastructure, legal environments, and social norms will evolve, and the world will become a very different and dramatically more productive place".

The revolution will be mobilized

It's clear that the future of the web is tied to smartphones and tablets and other mobile devices. More and more, people who visit your website will do so from a small-screened device instead of a hulking desktop or laptop.

An Asymco study found that people have adopted mobile phone technology faster than almost any other household technology.

What does that mean to you, the local business owner?

It means that if you want an effective web presence that supports your business goals, you need to have a website that supports a multitude of platforms, specifically the smartphone.

In fact, a study from Google found that that 6 in 10 mobile users will leave a website if it's not optimized for small screens.

If your business's site looks cramped, cluttered, or illegible when viewed on a tablet or smartphone, you run the very real risk of turning away your most valuable asset: your customers.

In a weak economy, mobile matters

Think this "mobile" stuff is much ado about nothing? Let's put this into perspective …

The economic recovery is a sluggish one. People are still worrying about losing their jobs. Millions of homeowners owe more on their mortgage loans than what their homes are worth. Credit-card debt continues to weigh down U.S. households.

These are challenging times for consumers. As a business owner, you don't want to give them any more reasons not to buy your products or services. Further, you don't want to add any additional friction to the process of buying your products and services!

A streamlined website for mobile is a new must-have. Particularly when you consider that people with smartphones are still turning to search engines to look for information.

Search to purchase

What's more, studies show that when people use their smartphones to search for information, they're more apt to take immediate action. They search from where they are and go immediately to what they find.

According to research from Mobile Marketer, 70 percent of all mobile searches result in action *within one hour!*

How does your website look and perform on a small screen?
What kind of experience are you providing to would-be buyers?

[ ] Good user experience

[ ] So-so user experience

[ ] Poor user experience

What all of this means to YOU!

Alright, let me ask you this:

- Do you search online before deciding what businesses to buy from?
- Do you choose a company based on the recommendations you heard from friends over social media?
- Do you carry a smartphone with you at all times?

We all do!

And again, these trends are only accelerating.

As much as we might wish they'd go away and let us continue with business as usual … the search/social/mobile paradigm is not going anywhere. It's here to stay.

The important thing now is to ask the hard questions and seek out the answers—even if they shake things up a bit:

- How do these changes impact the way consumers interact with my business?
- How do these changes impact my business's growth?
- How do these changes impact the way I approach the marketing of my business?

Chp 2: Dramatic Change Calls For A Renewed Focus On the Fundamentals!

The companies that get it, the firms that understand this and know just how to optimize how they work with these three factors are destroying the firms that do not.

So, the big question for you is do you work with these three big drivers of change to make sure that you come out on top in your industry?

It means that now more than ever you must truly have a promotion plan that works.
When I talk to small business they say man, there's so much going on. There's so much technology out there.

There's so much change occurring so quickly. It is not like I have time to sit around and study this stuff and work on this stuff all day every day. Just how do I keep up? Just how do I make conclusions about what I should do at my company?

Given all of these revolutionary changes we've discussed—search, social and mobile—you might be asking yourself the same questions and worried that you are going to have to make drastic, revolutionary changes in your business.

That's not necessarily the case.

Our experience shows that **there are four key marketing systems that need to be optimized in order to maximize growth** in today's wired, always-on and hyper-competitive marketplace.

The marketing systems we're about to present aren't even new!

They're not hifalutin' gimmicks that were cooked up in the ivory tower or by some pie-in-the-sky TED-talk guru.

They're proven concepts that have been tested, re-tested and tested again in the marketplace.

Now, sure, some of the tactics have changed, but the strategies themselves haven't.

As it happens, these four essential areas all start with the letter "R."

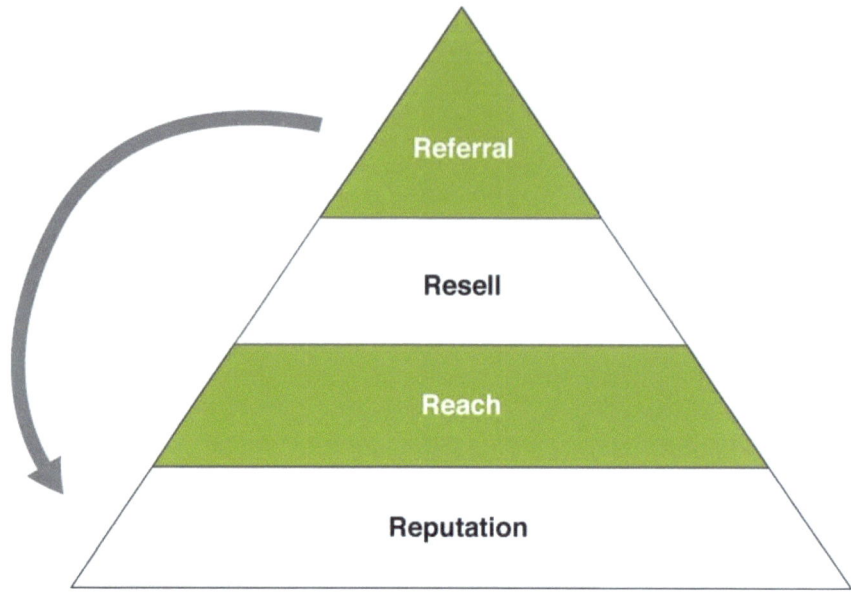

- **Reputation**
- **Reach**
- **Resell**
- **Referral**

These are the four things *every* business needs to plan for and optimize to maximize their growth potential.

It is merely a very simple pyramid. You can see what it is called the R-4 Marketing Framework. You will notice that arrow looping back around to the underside pointing back to Reputation and that's an important arrow.

The notion behind this pyramid is the fact that at its base is Reputation. Reputation is what folks think about our businesses and about us, services and products. Now, all of us know that reputation has consistently been important in company, but it's now more significant than ever.

We'll explain why, but the major reason why is because it's never been more easy for individuals to share what they feel about your company online. That information about your reputation, those feelings about your reputation and the way you deliver your products and services can now spread like wildfire.

Reach is making sure that you're getting in contact with more of your qualified prospects each and every day. It's rather obvious that in the event you would like to grow your company you should get more of your targeted prospects to understand who you're. If they do not know who you are they can't purchase from you Reach is the process and the systems we use to get in touch with more prospects and let them know about our business.

Then there is Resell. Resell, upsell and cross-sell to optimize the lifetime value of customer or a client.

Then, eventually, there is Referral and all of US know how valuable referrals are. We are getting out there in the marketplace that would be the simplest and best solution to grow our business, if we could just grow our business through referrals, through all the favorable word of mouth.

Sadly, that's usually not enough, but there are often times so much more we can do if we're thoughtful and proactive about our strategy to create referrals within our business.

 The idea behind it, again, is keeping it simple, keeping it focused.

Data shows, and my experience proves, that *each of these can account for about 25 percent growth on their own, and combined have a compounding effect that can ignite growth to 100 percent or more*.

Let's briefly run through each element and explore how maximizing these 4 R's could significantly impact growth at your business.

R1 Reputation

What are you doing to proactively manage, protect and monetize your most valuable asset—your reputation?

The first R is **reputation**. As we discussed earlier, it has never been easier for potential customers to find out what others think about your business. This is both good and bad (depending on what people find).

There is a rationale that Reputation is at the base of that pyramid. I really do consider it is the basis of marketing going forward. Why is that?
Well, it's simpler than ever for consumers to find the feedback of other consumers to help them make a determination about who to purchase from and you'll see all kinds of websites out there that rate companies.

There are the Yelps of the planet. Google actually has standings built into its search engine. I showed Trip Advisor to you before. There are all types of methods for individuals to review companies and review products and services and learn what others think.

The truth is, 70% of consumers say that the opinions they find online is the number two factor in making a choice about who visit to work with, or buy from. Share them with friends, family and colleagues.

The reality is that everyone is out there talking. The inquiry is what are they and who's talking about you? Make no mistake, they're discussing.

I enjoy the title of this publication from Pete Blackshaw Filled Customers Tell Upset Customers Tell 3,000, Three Pals. You may have discovered something along the lines before that a dissatisfied or angry customer would tell 10 people for each one person that a satisfied customer would tell.

Well, now because of social media negative feelings and those reviews are really simple to pass around that the unhappy customer get on the social media sites, will get online and tell thousands of their closest strangers on the net.

So, folks are talking about you and they're referring to your organization. Who?

A sample of who's talking about your business:
- Customers
- Prospects
- Competitors
- Disgruntled employees
- Ex spouses
- Former business partners, investors
- Trolls (the permanently aggrieved)

These really are the people that just want to get online and beat up companies it appears for no good reason.

This is really a copy of a TechCrunch article saying 'Google acquires Zagat to flush out local reviews.'

I'm sure you're all familiar with the Zagat guys, the novels that were published to review restaurants, pubs and hotels all over the entire world.

For individuals traveling to a brand new city these men were indispensable for a long time. Well, the value they had was all of these other people's evaluations, consumers and reviews captured in this publication in order that if you were traveling to another city for the first time you could find the places you thought would be far better go visit and kind of lower your own risk of getting lost in this new city and ending up in the wrong areas.

Well, Google realized that that was the most crucial information they could present to searchers to assist them make their buying choices. It was the opinions of other individuals and there is good reason behind that.

 All of us trust those recommendations we get from family and friends, but look at this. Seventy percent of online consumers trust unknown users, individuals we do not even understand, while just 14% of online consumers trust advertisements, so there is a tremendous gap between the marketing we are doing to get customers and how individuals trust that vs. the reviews of other individuals. That's why Zagat was bought by Google and is now incorporating reviews at the center of their search engines.

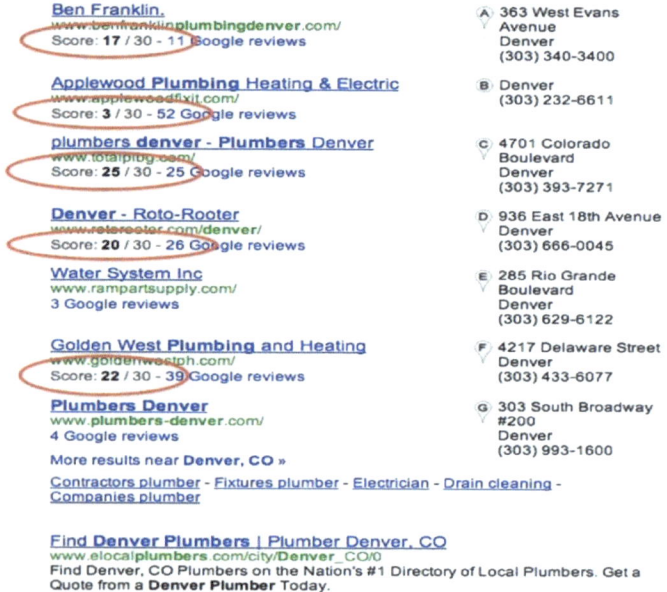

It is a screen shot I did. As you know, in case you do an internet search for any business in Google or any kind of company like Denver pizza restaurants, Denver plumbers or anything like this, you'll see these local reviews. The local reviews will have the local companies there in that category. They'll have the addresses and phone numbers. There'll be an image of a map to show you where they're located, but what is most significant is this. Everything I've circled in red there's a review score of these businesses based in the reviews of previous customers of that business.

Now, what's really, really frightening and this is the next pipes firm, Applewood Plumbing, Heating & Electric. They spend an awful lot of money on advertising in the Denver region. You can see by things like that and all the advertisements, so they're spending lots of money. Nevertheless, have a look at the review score that Applewood has from previous customers. Previous customers have a three out of 30 on 52 reviews. That, by any measure, is a failing grade, three out of 30.

So, they're spending all of that money on advertising to drive people mainly because people search in the search engines, to the search engines until they make a choice to purchase, and what do they see?

They see that the far majority of the previous customers of Applewood that left a review and have gone on here are completely dissatisfied with the service they received from

Applewood. I believe that you can see now why I say that reputation is the foundation of advertising going forward.

It does not matter what Applewood Plumbing does with their advertising at this point, all they're doing is driving people to see the negative reviews about their business. How would you feel here were the reviews that you discovered, poor to fair, poor to fair, poor to fair and if you went and searched about this company?

They are mainly just beating up Applewood Plumbing for inferior service, should you read the particulars of the reviews. Poor Applewood Plumbing, no matter what it does with the remainder of its own promotion, no matter how nicely it does with those other three R's is going to run head on into a serious problem growing their company due to their poor standing.

Your aim is to ensure you've a five star reputation at your company. That should be your first goal is to ensure that you have a five-star standing at your business. Now, how do you do that?

Well, I believe the most important and controllable thing you can do besides, of course, ensuring that you deliver excellent services and products which you certainly ought to be focused on, the next thing to do is to give, add to the dialog about your company in a meaningful way.

I mean that you simply can't control what folks are saying about your company, that is largely up to the person. Regardless how great of a job you do with your products and services some individuals are going to say negative things. It's only a fact of life of being in business, however you can be sure you're adding enough good content to the conversation that is taking place online to insure that the proportion of positive content out there vs. negative content out there's in your benefit.

What I mean by that is you should strategically ensure you are getting content online that is encouraging of your brand and favorable about your brand in order that when a consumer does do a search they locate great things about your organization instead of only a bunch of lousy reviews.

The very first step to doing this is to take ownership of the profiles in all of your key directories and networks. What I mean by directories and networks, I am talking about sites like Yelp, as I mentioned before, LinkedIn, the Google Plus local listings I just showed you a minute ago are absolutely most important since those are part of the Google search engine, but based on what company you are in maybe a site like Trip Advisor, certainly Facebook, Twitter, things like that.

You want to be sure that you own a company existence in which you have to have it, that you have taken control of that existence and that you're making sure the advice that's in these listings and directory sites is accurate and complete. You might not even recognize it, but you need a company listing in just about all of these sites already and a lot more.

The Superpages, the Yellow Pages sites online, they have all created listings about just about every company out there, but if you haven't taken control of it that means the info on there could possibly be wrong and maybe incomplete.

You may be receiving poor reviews from customers up there and not even having an opportunity to respond to them, so you need to take possession of these profiles to be sure that you can command the message that is on there and that is exactly what you would like to do.

You want to publish your own story about your business. You would like to create your own news. You want to post on good, positive, helpful subjects that'll help your clients, customers and prospects and you want to add social media sharing buttons to all of that content to make sure individuals can spread the good word about your business. How can you do that?

Make education videos and post them to YouTube. Video is very strong. Video is continuing to grow at merely an absolutely amazing rate. Look at this statistic. Any video that is given stands about a 50 times better likelihood of appearing on the very first page of results in the search engines than any given text page. That is since the search engines are smart. They've seen that searchers who find a video are generally much more engaged with that content than they're with text and analyzed the data.

People like to watch videos more than they like to read, so a growing number of videos are being shown by the search engines in the search engines to be relevant to what individuals are looking for. If you're able to create content about your company, which I am telling you any business can create great video content to share with their customers, creating video content gives you a real leg up in the various search engines and is an excellent solution to connect with your prospects and customers.

Next, you should build a reviews collecting system for your business. You don't need to simply leave it to chance that people will give favorable reviews about your company. You want to be certainly proactive and methodical about getting positive reviews and referrals at your company and make certain those things are becoming printed online.

There is a fascinating stat here. Conversion can be boosted by reviews on a website by 20%, which only means when people find a positive review they are likely to buy something or contact you when they see that positive review and if they go to your website. Thus, you want to be sure you are proactive in capturing the feelings of favorable happy customers and making certain that those feelings get shared.

The big takeaway here is that, reputation is currently the foundation of effective advertising. It is no longer enough to do good work and it is no longer enough to have great products and services. Those matters, of course, are important, but you have to develop and market your standing online. You have to make sure that those great feelings about your services and products and company end up so that other folks can locate them.
This probably isn't anything new to you, and there's a decent chance that, like most of the businesses I talk to, you are not very pleased about some of the things people have written about your business!

This brings up a larger point:

Whether it is positive or negative in tone, **most of the content about your business that is available online is not even being created by you anymore!**

Consumers are critics and publishers now. They all carry tiny "printing presses" in their pockets!

Reputation: more important than ever

To be sure, businesses have always relied on their reputation.

But the stakes are even higher today because of how easy it is for consumers to find information about local companies before they buy.

What's more, as we've already discussed, negative reviews can get lodged in the search results, hanging like an albatross around your neck and dragging down sales.

Are you "Googleable"? How many pages of Google are you on? (You may include Search, Maps, and Google+ Local citations in your answer)

[ ] Don't know
[ ] 0
[ ] 1
[ ] 2–5
[ ] 6+

Study: 90 percent of consumers online trust recommendations from people they know; seventy percent trust opinions of <u>unknown</u> users.

R2: Reach

What are you doing to ensure that more people know about you today than yesterday?

The second R is **reach**. It's my experience that *a business that wants to grow needs to make sure that more people know about it today than did yesterday*.

Now, when you've got that positive standing, as I said, you want to be certain that you're reaching out to as many prospects as you are able to in order to let them know the good word about your services and products. If you are not reaching out to more prospects daily then the odds of you growing your company long term are fairly slim to none.

There are obviously a variety of methods to reach customers and your target prospects. There are tons of ways, but we are going to dive in to a couple here starting with social media.
Social Media -- Since then the growth has just now been ridiculously quick.

There are now 155 million plus Facebook users in the U.S. and over 1 billion throughout the world. Social media giant Facebook is one of the biggest states on earth--
Chances are no matter who your market is that can reach them on Facebook.

I know lots of you probably don't think that Facebook is a workable marketing chance for you, but I hope to challenge you on that because I have seen Facebook work in just about every industry out there. So, let us talk about six reasons to market on Facebook.

1. Reach

As I said, just a gigantic number of individuals are on social media websites, particularly Facebook. You can reach huge amounts of every group of Facebook, every type of person out there, and consumer out there and social media give you multiple approaches to participate with them. So, again, whatever business you are in, whatever group you're going after, 's'm confident you can reach them on Facebook. Next is--

2. Precision Targeting

Facebook's advertising interface is completely amazing. If you have never run ads in there you really should jump in there simply to see. You can target individuals by place, including zip codes and area codes, by age, birthday, instruction, and not merely instruction like they were a school graduate. You can target particular classes at particular universities.

You can target people based on the connection they have, predicated on their demographic advice, predicated on psychographic information and their interests, even on things like their relationship standing. It's possible for you to get really, truly accurate in how you target people in Facebook.

3.Cost Control

Cost control is super important, especially for small businesses. You can advertise for as few as $20-$25 a day on Facebook. You can control how much you spend for each effort. That's space two, number four here--

4. Cost Efficiency

Thus, you have that precision targeting, you additionally have an incredible level of measurability.
Everything in online advertising you're doing may be quantified, which means that it may be optimized.

5. Simplicity

Facebook, in particular, is very easy to use. It's a great user interface which makes it merely a real wind to set up and get going. If you have used Google Adwords in yesteryear it is much, much simpler than that a nice and very simple advertising platform. Subsequently one of the matters that are most powerful, perhaps the strongest thing about advertising on Facebook, is this idea of...

6. Interest Targeting

Typically, in advertising what you can do is to target people by demographic information, where they dwell, how old they are, how much income they make, matters like that, but marketing starts to become a lot more powerful when you can reach folks predicated on their interests.

I mean everybody that's in Facebook posts everything about their life in there, the things they like, the things they don't enjoy, the areas they enjoy to go visit. All that good stuff gets posted in Facebook, so you can now customize your marketing to actually target that advice, which just makes it truly, extremely powerful.

I want to share with you one of the most effective ways to market on Facebook that each company should be taking advantage of and these are called Sponsored Story Ads.

Sponsored Story Advertisements show the ads to friends of that user and essentially convert a user's activity into advertisements. That's a mouthful, so I want to clarify my meaning. You'll probably locate one of the Sponsored Stories in your feed within a minute or two, should you hop on your Facebook account. You can see here in this instance, Jessica Gronski was at Starbucks and enjoyed Starbucks. Well, Starbucks paid that to turn into an ad to reveal all of Jessica's friends that she enjoyed Starbucks.

Any time you enjoy something on Facebook that can be turned into an ad and shown to your network of buddies on Facebook. Why would Starbucks need to do that? Well, because Starbucks understands that Jessica and her pals have things in common.

Starbucks understands that her friends should show that Jessica liked Starbucks to all her friend and family and most likely they're going to get others to enjoy Starbucks as well.

These Sponsored Narrative Ads generally are geared to improve the enjoys for your company, so if you have a Facebook profile for your business there then you can get likes from more folks. It's a genuinely nice advertising vehicle because it tightly fits in to how people use Facebook. It does not really show up as this big advertising, it just kind of fits into the remaining things that are exhibited in your stream.

Most importantly, you are now targeting individuals predicated on psychographics vs. only demographics, as we talked about before. Jessica and her pals will tend to get interests in common, that is what friends do, so you're now getting the benefit of targeting, specifically, other folks that have similar psychographic profiles as the man who just enjoyed your page.
This really is incredibly strong.

In reality, Facebook Sponsored Narratives have cost per lover than direct advertisements --

--and they've a 53% higher click-through rate than direct ads. So, it is a really strong type of advertising and it is strong, as I said, based on this particular notion that you are discussing somebody's specific experience with your brand with other people who are a lot more likely to enjoy your brand as well than just the general people that you'd be marketing to, so the advertisements end up being much, far more effective. This is a powerful and really, very simple type of advertising you can make the most of on Facebook.

The big takeaway here is your audience actually is socially active online who you are targeting. If you're not reaching them via social media I'm telling you that your adversaries are. This is really a simple form of advertising. It's very accessible, very simple to do, doesn't take a lot of cash and isn't very time consuming, so you all should be taking advantage of it.

Then let's talk about reach via mobile. As I said previously, mobile may be the largest game changer of the three major variables, Mobile, Social and Search. Let us talk about why that's.
 That amount looks light to me and it is likely because I am one of these folks here.

People are referred to by them as having nomophobia, that is the fear of being out of mobile phone contact.

Of smartphone subscribers confess to sleeping with their phones and I need to admit I'm one of these people. Mobile phones and smartphones actually have become something that folks only have attached to the hip reaching people via mobile is amazingly important, particularly if you are running a company that's local in nature.

One in three mobile searches are local in nature, which simply means that they're looking for the pizza shop or the local restaurant and trying to find the phone number or driving directions.

Six in 10 possibilities have said they will leave your site if it's not mobile friendly and --

52% of users say a poor mobile experience makes them much less inclined to participate with a business, which means that your aim is to have a mobile friendly site that could easily be found and the information on it be easily accessed.

This is a good example of a cellular site that is difficult. It's difficult to read, it's difficult to navigate and, sadly, this really comes from a website designer, which is not a good sign.

Here are a couple good examples of ways to make a mobile site accessible and much more simple to use.

It's possible for you to see in the left hand side here's this website called Howdah Layouts. This was their before picture. It's possible for you to see lots of little text there and simply littered and incredibly difficult to browse through and actually understand what you're looking at vs. on the right is their redesign where they are taking advantage of these big buttons and clear images and very, very limited text to make it very easy for someone to navigate through their website.

You wish to do the same for your organization. You want to make sure you are easily discovered on mobile devices because so many searches are currently taking place on cellular devices.

You've got to make sure that your website is ready to be looked at by those searchers that are mobile or you're missing out on a whole lot of consumer visibility.

So, the big takeaway here, consumers don't want to be disconnected from their telephones. You are given a chance to remain joined to consumers wherever they go by this dependence. You've got the chance to reach your audience without making consumers step out of their daily routines.

Do you have a method to build a continually growing prospect/client email list?
[ ] Yes
[ ] No
[ ] We don't have a list

R3: Resell

What are you doing to upsell, cross sell and repeat sell to maximize the lifetime value of your customer base?

All right, the third R is Resell. Again, that actually encompasses reselling, up selling and cross-selling, anything you're doing there to be sure that when you get a customer you are optimizing the lifetime value of that customer.

Whatever metaphor you want to use ... mining your backyard ... picking the low hanging fruit ... the point is the same:

It makes more sense (both financially and from an efficiency standpoint) to fully capitalize on your existing customer base than to be constantly on the hunt for new customers.

The more value you can generate from each customer, the less you have to spend on marketing, which means you can increase your profit margins and/or reinvest the savings into your products and services—in the process making your business even more attractive to your customers!

In practice, this can mean increasing the dollar value of each transaction or increasing the frequency that customers buy, either by offering add-on services or upsells or cross-sells.

McDonald's offers the classic example: 'Do you want fries with that?' 'Do you want to supersize your order?'

These days there are so many cost effective and trackable ways to bring customers back to your business.

To give you just one example, consider SMS coupon campaigns. With monthly costs lower than $30 to send 1000 text messages, and average redemption rates of 20 percent or more, it potentially costs less than 30 cents per customer in your door!

Despite having easy access to new and cool tools, most business in our area are leaving money on the table because they're not maximizing the resell potential of each customer.

Thus, let's talk about resell via cellular telephone again real fast.

Cellular Telephone, as I mentioned, may be the largest factor of the three that we have to be paying attention to. Eighty-seven percent of Americans have mobile phones. Seventy-three percent say it is mobilephones one most used technology apparatus. I know I did several years back. Mobile has only become part of our culture.

Well, I think SMS text messaging is among the strongest ways that I've seen to date and can be used by so many companies. SMS messages are only those text messages which you send and receive on your cellphone. SMS text messages are capable of reaching 91% of the U.S. population because that's a capability that is built in to nearly every single mobile phone that's made.

Well, instant deliverability. Those messages will immediately arrive. It's a very flexible, simple- to-use platform. Your consumers have really easy ways to opt-in and opt-out. They are able to get off your list should they actually do not need it, so make sure to are playing by the rules. There are quite high open and conversion rates. Meaning, just about everybody opens their SMS messages on what they find and they take action. SMS messages are very, very low attempt to make and send. It's super simple, just a little bit of text.

The reality is, those reasons to use SMS that I just mentioned, the outcomes are super powerful. Compare that to email. We all should understand the ability of email marketing. Email marketing is just a gigantic, huge business generator, but 33% of email addresses change on a yearly basis, which makes it hard to stay in touch with people via e-mail, in case you do not.

Should you look at the open rates for electronic mail, the average open rates for email are down now around five percent. Just five percent of emails actually get opened compared to 97% of all SMS marketing texts getting opened. So, it is simpler to reach them, it is a far better way to reach them.

Let us talk about a number of special ways that companies can use SMS. So, if you have any kind of business where you're reliant upon appointments, a dental office, a chiropractic office, a massage therapist, things like that where people set an appointment to visit your company, well, as you know, no shows are an enormous killer of profitability at your company. That is only an hour where you could have taken care of another paying customer, you have wasted if people don't show up for their appointment.

SMS reminders sent to people's phones prior to their appointment are demonstrated to lessen no-shows by 50% or more, meaning you are able to save a lot of cash and put it back in your business or into your pocket. SMS reminders delivered right to those cellphones are a really good approach to get people to appear for their appointments.

Mobile coupons are another really strong type of advertising that almost all businesses are able to make the most of. Mobile coupons are 10 times more likely to be redeemed than traditional coupons, so you are getting individuals to take a lot more action than conventional print coupons with cellular coupons and then geotargeting.
Geotargeting means that you can automatically send text coupons to folks when they're within the neighborhood of a particular geographic location. How strong is that?

If somebody is within five miles of your pizza shop, let us say, you can send a message saying hey, you are close to them. So, how strong is this? I mean it really is just astounding that you may actually target individuals based on where they're at. It doesn't have to be only your business. Imagine if people are within five miles of a competition? Maybe that is when you would like to send them your ad to get them to pay attention to you instead of the competitor they were getting close to or your coupon.

Text messaging is super, super powerful. It's the most popular type of communicating among consumers on electronic devices as well as your audience is almost guaranteed to get and to read your SMS text message. Every business should start assembling their text list now so they can learn more about the advertising opportunities which are out there via SMS text.

The more value you can generate from each customer, the less you have to spend on marketing, which means you can increase your profit margins and/or reinvest the savings into your products and services—in the process making your business even more attractive to your customers!

Do you ethically (but effectively) prepare buyers from their very first purchasing experience with you to keep coming back to purchase over and over again?
[ ] No
[ ] Yes
[ ] Not sure

R4: Referral

What are you doing to use your successful relationships to create new, organic opportunities so that you can spend less and make more?

All right, the fourth R is Referral. Again, referral is getting those joyful customers share the good word about your products, service as well as your own business to other prospects in the marketplace and to say great things about you.

Since you're doing such a great job taking care of your customers and keeping them happy, the next best thing you can do is set up systems to maximize the benefit you get from them, right? So that they are doing the marketing for you!

It's well known that ***if you just leave it up to people to do referrals for you, very few will—even if they are very happy with you***.

You have to make it very easy—almost effortless—for your happy customers to refer your business if you really want to maximize the referrals you generate from them.

A study from Lee Resource Inc. found that attracting a new customer can cost five times as much as keeping an existing one.

This is actually the easiest method to get new customers, when you get good hot referrals and you get those people to come in that are already purchased. We'd all take as many of these as we can possibly get.

--41% of companies count on referrals for over 80% of their sales. So, referrals are unbelievably important.

The inquiry is how can you proactively drive instead of just expecting the come to you personally, referrals?

One of my favourite expressions in business is that hope is not a strategy. We want to have a proactive approach instead of merely expecting we'll get more to drive more referrals. To do that you must understand that great customer service does not always equate to referrals.

Eighty-three percent of satisfied clients are willing to send services and products, but only 29% really do. Why is that? Well, it does not actually matter the reason why.

What matters is that you have to leverage a proactive referral system if you are going to get more of these referrals. You clearly can not simply leave the consumers it because even though 83% say they'd, only 29% actually do.

Word of mouth relies off of likelihood vs. a referral system which is something that's predictable, consistent and repeatable that you control.

A referral system is a methodical process that captures qualified prospects through your association with individuals. So, how do you create a repeatable system as well as referrals?

The simple answer is that you ask for qualified prospects.

Ninety-one percent of customers would give a referral, but have never been inquired. Most of us simply don't take the time to actually request individuals to share their feelings with family and their friends about their experience with your company and your products or services.

It is actually fairly clear-cut. So, I want to share with you a few examples.

Here is a direct mail piece. It says 'Hey, turkey, give thanks to yourself with some free months.' This merely says 'Refer some friends to the Dollar Shave Club and you will get a complimentary month of Dollar Shave Club shavers for each friend that you just sign up.' Any company can take advantage of this simple. This only comes inside their bundle when they razors come to your residence.

You could also do this internet. Incorporate referral requests on social networking pages such as this one from REI on Facebook and into coupons, competitions and other viral promotions on your website so that the great things that people say about you can virally be spread to others.

All right, the huge takeaway. Referrals are excellent, but are difficult to depend on if you can't make them predictable, so it is your job to design a repeatable system that captures the referrals when your customers are thrilled. When they're happy you want to take advantage of that by giving them a simple vehicle to share those positive feelings with others, and that means you just have to inquire and you just must make it as easy as possible.

Referrals make great customers

We all want referrals because they help us save money on marketing, right?

Well, there's even more to gain from referrals than cost savings:

According to a case study noted in the Harvard Business Review, customers that come from referrals are, on average, about 18 percent more likely than others to stay with a company and they generate 16 percent more in profits!

And according to several case studies reported on by the website TechCrunch:

Friends referred by friends make better customers.

They spend more (a 2x higher estimated lifetime value than customers from all other channels at One Kings Lane); **convert better** (75 percent higher conversion than renters from other marketing channels at Rent the Runway); and **shop faster** (they make their first purchase after joining twice as quickly than referrals from other channels at Trendyol).

Why are referrals so powerful?

Because they channel the power of **social proof**. Social proof is a fancy way of saying that we humans are easily influenced by each other.

We're pack animals.

When a member of our pack (family) or tribe (social circle) recommends a product or service, we take that recommendation very seriously.

Similarly, when someone in a position of power, prestige or authority recommends something, we are very **quick to act** on that recommendation.

You see the applied power of social proof everywhere: in TV ads, when you see a celebrity endorsing a product; on the radio, when the person hosting the pledge drive tells listeners that so-and-so donated $50 to NPR; on the back of a novel you're reading, when you see testimonials from other notable authors; and on the web, when you visit sites like Yelp.com to read consumer reviews of local restaurants.

Moving from passive to active, ad hoc to systematic

Almost without fail, **most businesses I talk to have no clear referral generation system**.

They essentially think that referrals are something that you simply wait and hope for … but **the reality is that referrals don't just happen, you have to go out and get them!**

And if you're going to spend the time collecting them, you need a system that effectively channels your efforts into tangible results.

Chp 3: What are you missing?

Now, the problem is that most businesses are operating without even being aware of these changes or marketing systems, and how it is impacting their business.

Let me show you some examples …

First, if you aren't effectively and proactively managing your reputation, you aren't aware of comments like this being made about your business:

Ouch. That hurts. Comments like these will negatively impact how others view your business in the marketplace. According to Nielsen, user reviews are "the most trusted form of advertising."

Or, you have people looking for your business on their mobile phones, and your website is showing like this:

No one has fingers small enough (or patience long enough) to navigate this web page. A study from Google found that 60 percent of users will leave a website if it's not optimized for mobile.

While your competitors' mobile website is showing up like this:

People will stay on your competitor's website if it's optimized for a small touchscreen.

So, how can we address some of these things?

Let me share some ideas … I obviously can't give you all of them in the space of this small book, but let me share a few:

- Control your own reviews with your own review site
- Create a separate mobile site for your business that is optimized for mobile
- Reach more people more cost-effectively and with greater targeting using Facebook ads

Is your business being left behind?

Now, if you fall into the category of businesses that are not proactively working with these technology changes and marketing systems, **you are only going to see things get worse over time**.

These changes, though recent, are now a permanent part of the competitive landscape.

The gap between the businesses that "get it" and those that don't is widening at an accelerating pace.

You can look at any industry and see examples of the handful of businesses that are really pulling away from the pack, and those that are falling behind.

It's time to go 'all-in'

Do you have someone that is helping your business in these areas?

Or are you kidding yourself into thinking that you are going to try to do this by yourself or with the very part-time effort of one of your employees that has no marketing background?

That's not going to cut it.

Do you watch "Parks and Recreation"? to paraphrase the wise Ron Swanson, *you can't half-ass two things. You've got to whole-ass one thing.*

If you're struggling to fit everything into your calendar already (most business owners I talk to are), you're probably not going have the bandwidth to optimize the four R's. Either something else has to give, or you need to enlist a friendly expert to help you!

Answer the call

Get this: according to data from Google, **61 percent of local searches on a mobile phone result in a phone call**.

Are you ready, both literally and figuratively, to answer that call?

Or are you going to let ring until one of your competitors picks up the phone?

Are you ready to answer the call? Or are you going to let ring until one of your competitors picks up the phone?

Chp 4: Take Your Inventory: What Are You Doing to Optimize the Four R's?

Reputation: What are you doing to proactively manage, protect and monetize your most valuable asset—your reputation?

_____

_____

_____

_____

_____

_____

Reach: What are you doing to ensure that more people know about you today than yesterday?

_____

_____

_____

_____

_____

_____

Resell: _What are you doing to upsell, cross sell and repeat sell to maximize the lifetime value of your customer base?_

_____

_____

_____

_____

_____

_____

Referral: _What are you doing to use your successful relationships to create new, organic opportunities so that you can spend less and make more?_

_____

_____

_____

_____

_____

_____

I hope you can see that just by focusing on these four places, maximizing and optimizing these four places, we can take our company to drastically higher levels of growth.

The far majority of times once i ask that question the answer is no. Well, again, we're small businesses, we're resource constrained. Many times it is just lack of knowledge of the alternatives that are accessible to you or it is too little time or budget or just work force and expertise there at your organization. You are busy creating whatever service or product it's the fact that you do for a living and you also don't have enough time to think about or implement all of these new marketing strategies and systems at your company.

Well, what's the problem with that?

The issue is the difference between those that really get it and are taking advantage of the internet marketing strategies, the technology, taking advantage of the search, societal along with the cellular that we discussed, well the difference between those that get that and those that don't is widening. The companies that are taking advantage of those three factors with proven advertising systems are beating their opposition.

I find that 90% recognize that small businesses out there about this topic and those that have gone through this presentation or something similar to it are n't growing like they should while I speak to them.

Almost every small business owner out there that I speak to says yeah, man, we should be doing more. We are not growing as fast as we'd like. It's been rough years. It's been a demanding economy. I'm not making the money I need to. That's a theme that is common amongst nearly every company owner that I discuss with, but only 50% of those folks realize they should make a change.

What I mean by that is many small business owners believe oh, it is the economy or somebody else has some product or service which provides a real edge to them and that's why they are not growing. Well, in most cases it's not the economy. It is not the services or products you are competing against. Every small business out there that I see has the chance to grow much quicker than small business are regardless of competitive powers or economic conditions.

The challenge is that it's you that's to make that change. You can not wait around for the economy to get better. That is the problem. Just 20% realize that being strategic about their advertising is the difference.

As I mentioned, it's not the products and services. Almost all of you have excellent products and services. It's not the market. In every industry right now there's a company that's growing like wildfire regardless of demanding economic conditions or a poor economy. It is not the economy. It's taking advantage of all the marketing systems and capabilities that are out there for your business to optimize to fuel your growth.

Therefore, if you are part of the 20% ....

The 20% that is completely dedicated to creating maximum increase at your business and comprehends that yeah, the economy may be tough, yeah, there might be tough competition out there, but really there are plenty of matters that I can command and that I should be doing better ... if you are one of those folks I'd like to get to know you as well as your business better.

If you're ready to make a shift ...

You may realize that you need to make a change, that you aren't growing like you should, that your current approach to marketing is not working, and that you are committed to getting past your current income limits.

If so, I would be interested in talking with you to see if there is potentially a good fit to work together because we are particular about who we work with.

We work with businesses that are already successful and are looking for strategic ways to get FAR MORE successful.

We work with clients that have the mindset and resources to handle the level of growth that is possible to achieve.

What to do next

If you've seen the benefit of what you've read in these pages, then I'd encourage you to contact us immediately. From there, we will set up a 30 minutes phone call interview to see if we are a good fit to work together.

This phone conversation is a free, no-obligation strategy session to see if we're a good fit for each other. It is a necessary first step if we are to work toward achieving the growth you're capable of!

How to contact us
Pick a method, any method:

Email: info@roarmarketingconsultants.com
Website: www.roarmarketingconsultants.com

Want to be a guest expert on one of our online shows?

Go to http://www.LocalExpertSpotLightTv.com

We look forward to hearing from you!